WHAT DIFFERENCE DOES JESUS MAKE?

The Tough Questions Series

**TOUGH
QUESTIONS**
REVISED EDITION

WHAT

DIFFERENCE

DOES JESUS

MAKE?

WHAT DIFFERENCE DOES JESUS MAKE?

JUDSON POLING
foreword by **Lee Strobel**

ZONDERVAN™
GRAND RAPIDS, MICHIGAN 49530 USA

WILLOW
Willow Creek Resources

ZONDERVAN.COM/
AUTHOR**TRACKER**

We want to hear from you. Please send your comments about this book to us in care of zreview@zondervan.com. Thank you.

ZONDERVAN™

What Difference Does Jesus Make?
Copyright © 1998, 2003 by Willow Creek Association

Formerly titled *Is Jesus the Only Way?*

Requests for information should be addressed to:

Zondervan, *Grand Rapids, Michigan 49530*

ISBN-10: 0-310-24503-6
ISBN-13: 978-0-310-24503-2

Interior design by Nancy Wilson

Printed in the United States of America

06 07 08 09 10 11 12 • 20 19 18 17 16 15 14 13 12 11 10 9 8 7 6 5 4

Contents

Foreword

For most of my life I was an atheist. I thought that the Bible was hopelessly riddled with mythology, that God was a man-made creation born of wishful thinking, and that the deity of Jesus was merely a product of legendary development. My no-nonsense education in journalism and law contributed to my skeptical viewpoint. In fact, just the idea of an all-powerful, all-loving, all-knowing creator of the universe seemed too absurd to even justify the time to investigate whether there could be any evidence backing it up.

However, my agnostic wife's conversion to Christianity, and the subsequent transformation of her character and values, prompted me to launch my own spiritual journey in 1980. Using the skills I developed as the legal affairs editor of *The Chicago Tribune,* I began to check out whether any concrete facts, historical data, or convincing logic supported the Christian faith. Looking back, I wish I had this curriculum to supplement my efforts.

This excellent material can help you in two ways. If you're already a Christ-follower, this series can provide answers to some of the tough questions your seeker friends are asking—or you're asking yourself. If you're not yet following Christ but consider yourself either an open-minded skeptic or a spiritual seeker, this series can also help you in your journey. You can thoroughly and responsibly explore the relevant issues while discussing the topics in community with others. In short, it's a tremendous guide for people who really want to discover the truth about God and this fascinating and challenging Nazarene carpenter named Jesus.

If the previous paragraph describes you in some way, prepare for the adventure of a lifetime. Let the pages that follow take you on a stimulating journey of discovery as you grapple with the most profound—and potentially life-changing—questions in the world.

—Lee Strobel, author of
The Case for Christ and *The Case for Faith*

Getting Started

Welcome to the Tough Questions series! This small group curriculum was produced with the conviction that claims regarding spiritual truth can and should be tested. Religions—sometimes considered exempt from scrutiny—are not free to make sweeping declarations and demands without providing solid reasons why they should be taken seriously. These teachings, including those from the Bible in particular, purport to explain the most significant of life's mysteries, with consequences alleged to be eternal. Such grand claims should be analyzed carefully. If this questioning process exposes faulty assertions, it only makes sense to refuse to place one's trust in these flawed systems of belief. If, on the other hand, an intense investigation leads to the discovery of truth, the search will have been worth it all.

Christianity contends that God welcomes sincere examination and inquiry; in fact, it's a matter of historical record that Jesus encouraged such scrutiny. The Bible is not a secret kept only for the initiated few, but an open book available for study and debate. The central teachings of Christianity are freely offered to all, to the skeptic as well as to the believer.

So here's an open invitation: explore the options, examine the claims, and draw your conclusions. And once you encounter and embrace the truth—look out! Meaningful life-change and growth will be yours to enjoy.

> You will seek me and find me when you seek me with all your heart.
>
> —Jeremiah 29:13

It is possible for any of us to believe error; it is also feasible for us to resist truth. Using this set of discussion guides will help you sort out the true from the supposed, and ultimately offer a reasonable defense of the Christian faith. Whether you are a nonbeliever or skeptic, or someone who is already convinced and looking to fortify your faith, these guides will lead you to a fascinating exploration of vital spiritual truths.

Tough Questions for Small Groups

The Tough Questions series is specifically designed to give spiritual seekers (or non-Christians) a chance to raise questions and investigate the basics of the Christian faith within the safe context of a seeker small group. These groups typically consist of a community of two to twelve seekers and one or two leaders who gather on a regular basis, primarily to discuss spiritual matters. Seeker groups meet at a wide variety of locations, from homes and offices to restaurants and churches to bookstores and park district picnic tables. A trained Christian leader normally organizes the group and facilitates the discussions based on the seekers' spiritual concerns and interests. Usually, at least one apprentice (or coleader) who is also a Christian assists the group leader. The rest of the participants are mostly, if not all, non-Christians. This curriculum is intended to enhance these seeker small group discussions and create a fresh approach to exploring the Christian faith.

Because the primary audience is the not-yet-convinced seeker, these guides are designed to represent the skeptical, along with the Christian, perspective. While the truths of the Christian position are strongly affirmed, it is anticipated that non-Christians will dive into these materials with a group of friends and discover that their questions and doubts are not only well understood and represented here, but also valued. If that goal is accomplished, open and honest discussions about Christianity can follow. The greatest hope behind the formation of this series is that seekers will be challenged in a respectful way to seriously consider and even accept the claims of Christ.

A secondary purpose behind the design of this series is to provide a tool for small groups of Christians to use as they discuss answers to the tough questions seekers are asking. The process of wrestling through these important questions and issues will not only strengthen their own personal faith but also provide them with insights for entering into informed dialogues about Christianity with their seeking friends.

A hybrid of the two options mentioned above may make more sense for some groups. For example, a small group of Christians may want to open up their discussion to include those who are just beginning to investigate spiritual things. This third approach provides an excellent opportunity for both Christians and seekers to examine the claims of Christianity together. Whatever the configuration of your group, may you benefit greatly as you use these guides to fully engage in lively discussions about issues that matter most.

Guide Features

The Introduction

At the beginning of every session is an introduction, usually several paragraphs long. You may want to read this beforehand even though your leader will probably ask the group to read it aloud together at the start of every meeting. These introductions are written from a skeptical point of view, so a full spectrum of perspectives is represented in each session. Hopefully, this information will help you feel represented, understood, and valued.

Open for Discussion

Most sessions contain ten to fifteen questions your group can discuss. You may find that it is difficult for your group to get through all these questions in one sitting. That is okay; the important thing is to engage in the topic at hand—not to necessarily get through every question. Your group, however, may decide to spend more than one meeting on each session in order to address all of the questions. The Open for Discussion sections are designed to draw out group participation and give everyone the opportunity to process things openly.

Usually, the first question of each session is an "icebreaker." These simple questions are designed to get the conversation going by prompting the group to discuss a nonthreatening issue, usually having to do with the session topic to be covered. Your group may want to make time for additional icebreakers at the beginning of each discussion.

Heart of the Matter

The section called "Heart of the Matter" represents a slight turn in the group discussion. Generally speaking, the questions in this section speak more to the emotional, rather than just the intellectual, side of the issue. This is an opportunity to get in touch with how you feel about a certain aspect of the topic being discussed and to share those feelings with the rest of the group.

Charting Your Journey

The purpose of the "Charting Your Journey" section is to challenge you to go beyond a mere intellectual and emotional discussion to personal application. This group experience is, after all, a journey, so each session includes this section devoted to helping you identify and talk about your current position. Your views will most likely fluctuate as you make new discoveries along the way.

Straight Talk

Every session has at least one section, called "Straight Talk," designed to stimulate further thinking and discussion around relevant supplementary information. The question immediately following Straight Talk usually refers to the material just presented, so it is important that you read and understand this part before you attempt to answer the question.

Quotes

Scattered throughout every session are various quotes, many of them from skeptical or critical points of view. These are simply intended to spark your thinking about the issue at hand.

Recommended Resources

This section at the back of each guide lists recommended books that may serve as helpful resources for further study.

Discussion Guidelines

These guides, which consist mainly of questions to be answered in your group setting, are designed to elicit dialogue rather than short, simple answers. Strictly speaking, these guides are not Bible studies, though they regularly refer to biblical themes and passages. Instead, they are topical discussion guides, meant to get you talking about what you really think and feel. The sessions have a point and attempt to lead to some resolution, but they fall short of providing the last word on any of the questions raised. That is left for you to discover for yourself! You will be invited to bring your experience, perspective, and uncertainties to the discussion, and you will also be encouraged to compare your beliefs with what the Bible teaches in order to determine where you stand as each meeting unfolds.

Your group should have a discussion leader. This facilitator can get needed background material for each session in the *Tough Questions Leader's Guide.*

There, your leader will find some brief points of clarification and understanding (along with suggested answers) for many of the questions in each session. The supplemental book *Seeker Small Groups* is also strongly recommended as a helpful resource for leaders to effectively start up small groups and facilitate discussions for spiritual seekers. *The Complete Book of Questions: 1001 Conversation Starters for Any Occasion,* a resource filled with icebreaker questions, may be a useful tool to assist everyone in your group to get to know one another better, and to more easily launch your interactions.

In addition, keep the following list of suggestions in mind as you prepare to participate in your group discussions.

1. The Tough Questions series does not necessarily need to be discussed sequentially. The guides, as well as individual sessions, can be mixed and matched in any order and easily discussed independently of each other, based on everyone's interests and questions.

2. If possible, read over the material before each meeting. Familiarity with the topic will greatly enrich the time you spend in the group discussion.

3. Be willing to join in the group interaction. The leader of the group will not present a lecture but rather will encourage each of you to openly discuss your opinions and disagreements. Plan to share your ideas honestly and forthrightly.

4. Be sensitive to the other members of your group. Listen attentively when they speak and be affirming whenever you can. This will encourage more hesitant members of the group to participate. Always remember to show respect toward the others even if they don't always agree with your position.

5. Be careful not to dominate the discussion. By all means participate, but allow others to have equal time.
6. Try to stick to the topic being studied. There won't be enough time to handle the peripheral tough questions that come to mind during your meeting.
7. It would be helpful for you to have a good modern translation of the Bible, such as the New International Version, the New Living Translation, or the New American Standard Bible. You might prefer to use a Bible that includes notes especially for seekers, such as *The Journey: The Study Bible for Spiritual Seekers.* Unless noted otherwise, questions in this series are based on the New International Version.
8. Do some extra reading in the Bible and other recommended books as you work through these sessions. The "Recommended Resources" section at the back of each guide offers some ideas of books to read.

Unspeakable Love

Christianity stands or falls on Christ. Yet he left us with a whole lot of hard sayings. But the central scandal of Christianity is that at a point in history, God came down to live among us in a person, Jesus of Nazareth. And the most baffling moment of Jesus' life was on the cross, where he hung to die like a common criminal. In that place of weakness—where all seemed lost, where the taunts of "Prove yourself, Jesus, and come down from there!" lashed out like the whip that flogged him prior to his crucifixion—somehow God was at his best. There at the cross, he expressed a love greater than words could ever describe. That act of Jesus, presented as the ultimate demonstration of the love and justice of God, begs to be put to "cross" examination.

As you wrestle with these tough questions, be assured that satisfying, reasonable answers are waiting to be found. And you're invited to discover them with others in your small group as you explore and discuss these guides. God bless you on your spiritual journey!

Seek and you will find; knock and the door will be opened to you.

—Matthew 7: 7

What Difference Does Jesus Make?

Imagine a married man boasting, "I have the most beautiful wife in the world!" You might smile at the man's affection though behind his back you recognize his obvious romantic blindness. Such exaggeration is forgivable and is the stuff of good marriages—even though it's not reliable information about women.

Now picture that same man's wife walking up to you and stating, without the least hint of exaggeration, "I am the most beautiful woman in the world." You would most likely have an entirely different reaction, thinking that she was arrogant or at least terribly confused. *Who does she think she is, to expect me to believe that about her?* you might wonder. If she were to summon you to debate the claim, you might not know where to start—but you would definitely know she was wrong.

In the spiritual realm, the Bible claims that Jesus is more than just a way to God—he is *the* way. Are sincere Christians just exaggerating their love for their leader and teacher? If so, maybe we can forgive their zeal, because—as with the married man in the above example—it comes from an innocent, though misinformed, perspective.

But what if they're saying more? What if they know there are other options but won't consider any? Now the cry of religious bigotry is raised.

Or even one step further: What if Jesus himself claimed he alone is the way? As you'll see in the coming discussions, agree with him or not, it's impossible to deny that Jesus did believe some amazing things about himself.

Critics naturally reject these assertions of superiority. Philosopher and atheist Bertrand Russell wrote, "I cannot myself feel that either in the matter of wisdom or in the matter of virtue Christ stands quite as high as some other people known to history. I think I should put Buddha and Socrates above him in those respects" *(The Basic Writings of Bertrand Russell)*. In making this statement, Russell knew he was not just disagreeing with Christians—he was disagreeing with Jesus himself. Were we to further tease out the implications of what critics like Russell are saying, we would no longer be able to think of Jesus as simply a benign, wisdom-spouting sage. He would have to be considered crazy or at least dangerously deluded and full of himself. Jesus declared open season on all other religious teachers. The clear implication is that if you or anyone you know follows someone other than Jesus, Jesus would insist you follow him instead. In light of these statements, it's clear why he irritated so many of his contemporaries and why he continues to irritate people like Russell, and others who look into his teachings today.

Of course, the possibility that Jesus was right must be granted, if only for the sake of argument. Yet the result of accepting his sweeping claims about himself leaves us groping for answers to the questions that immediately follow: Where does that leave those who don't follow him? Where does that leave those who never had the chance to follow him? Has God really set up such an elite club? Why wouldn't God send a "Jesus" for each new generation and in multiple cultures? If Jesus was so wonderful, why send him only once?*

---

*For additional discussions about these questions see the Tough Questions book *Don't All Religions Lead to God?*

This guide will help you look at these outrageous claims—not from a woman trying to convince you of her beauty but from Jesus of Nazareth, who is trying to convince you of his deity. You be the judge of whether he's right and what is the right response for you to make.

Who Was Jesus?

Does Anybody Know for Sure?

It's been decades since President John F. Kennedy was assassinated, but people are still fascinated with his life—and death. One gets the impression that the further we are from the actual events, the bigger his life and reputation gets. There's an almost mythical quality to his thousand-day reign in American politics. Even the revelation of serious character flaws hasn't diminished many people's nostalgic interest.

What about the theories concerning his death? Serious, knowledgeable people seem divided about the exact number of bullets shot and about whether or not Lee Harvey Oswald acted alone. With so many eyewitnesses, how could the facts of such a famous assassination be so inconclusive?

People are just as divided in their opinions about Jesus. Maybe he was a great teacher who gathered a following centuries ago. But now, so many years later, how can we know who he really was? Over the years, perhaps the stories have grown. The "real" Jesus may be lost forever behind the curtain of historical obscurity.

On the other hand, what harm is there in thinking that Jesus is the Son of God—even if that idea is the product of religious leaders who exaggerated his influence long after he was gone? Does Jesus have to be God incarnate to be a good influence on humanity?

Christ may be said to be a fiction in the four senses that (1) it is quite possible that there was no historical Jesus; (2) even if there was, he is lost to us, the result being that there is no historical Jesus available to us; (3) the Jesus who "walks with me and talks with me and tells me I am his own" is an imaginative visualization and in the nature of the case can be nothing more than a fiction; and finally, (4) "Christ" as a corporate logo for this and that religious institution is a euphemistic fiction, not unlike Ronald McDonald, Mickey Mouse, or Joe Camel, the purpose of which is to get you to swallow a whole raft of beliefs, attitudes, and behaviors by an act of simple faith, short-circuiting the dangerous process of thinking the issues out to your own conclusions.

—Marshall J. Gauvin,
Did Jesus Christ Really Live?

Why can't we just be grateful for the good done by his teachings, without worrying about who he was or what he said about himself?

And even if we did have an accurate understanding of Jesus, what difference would it make today? He's been gone for two thousand years! The important thing is that we use what he (or his followers) left behind. Let his wisdom and counsel stand alongside that of all the other great teachers, like Confucius or the Buddha—why must we be pressed into being dogmatic about something so hard to prove? Leave theologizing to the experts. Let the words of Jesus be enjoyed for what they can do for us, and let's not quibble about whether they're true in any absolute sense. Right?

In short, what's all the fuss about Jesus' identity?

OPEN FOR DISCUSSION

1. What are some of the common things you have heard people say about who Jesus was?

2. From the list of words and phrases below, check the top three that sum up your current understanding of Jesus:

myth	leader	overrated
man	guru	rebel
nobody special	Son of God	misunderstood
teacher	prophet	King
idea	Lord	other: _____

3. What is one word or phrase from the previous list that you believe is not true about Jesus?

4. During our lives we have all accumulated "facts" about Jesus—some of which may not be entirely accurate. Which of the following have strongly influenced your picture about who Jesus was?

- an encyclopedia
- a modern theologian
- someone antagonistic toward Christianity
- a psychic
- a pastor or minister
- a really nice person
- a person who sounds very intelligent
- someone who claims to hear Jesus speak to them
- my mother or father
- friends
- a scientist
- someone who "channels" Jesus (or other spiritual entities)
- an idea that came to me while I was deep in thought
- a book I read
- TV or movies
- ancient documents written by people who actually knew Jesus or heard him speak

5. Choose one or two of the above sources of information. What are the strengths and weaknesses of relying on these sources?

STRAIGHT TALK

What the Gospels Say About Jesus

The most reliable information about any historical figure comes from records of those who knew the person — preferably from multiple sources. Such material about Jesus is contained in the ancient documents written by those who knew him (or who interviewed eyewitnesses). These records are called the Gospels and are titled after their authors: Matthew, Mark, Luke, and John. They were written in the first century, within the lifetime of those who knew Jesus personally or heard him speak. From these detailed histories, we can gather statements regarding what Jesus claimed about himself.

It is not necessary to believe that these documents are God's Word in order to acknowledge that, as historical sources, they are the best pieces of evidence we have, and that they are closer to the original events than any other source (certainly closer than a later author or modern interpreter). Therefore, if we find a trend or theme concerning what Jesus says about himself, we can at the very least acknowledge it's *his* perspective about himself. (Of course, he could have been wrong, but at least we have reliable records of his claims.)

6. Write a concise statement of Jesus' belief, based on information gleaned from the following passages. (Remember, you do not need to agree with what was said; just sum up what Jesus was trying to tell his audience about his identity).

[Jesus said,] "Whoever acknowledges me before men, I will also acknowledge him before my Father in heaven. But whoever disowns me before men, I will disown him before my Father in heaven. Do not suppose that I have come to bring peace to the earth. I did not come to bring peace, but a sword. For I have come to turn 'a man against his father, a daughter against her mother, a daughter-in-law against her mother-in-law—a man's enemies will be the members of his own household.' Anyone who loves his father or mother more than me is not worthy of me; anyone who loves his son or daughter more than me is not worthy of me; and anyone who does not take his cross and follow me is not worthy of me. Whoever finds his life will lose it, and whoever loses his life for my sake will find it."

—Matthew 10:32–39

Because Jesus was doing these things on the Sabbath, the Jews persecuted him. Jesus said to them, "My Father is always at his work to this very day, and I, too, am working." For this reason the Jews tried all the harder to kill him; not only was he breaking the Sabbath, but he was even calling God his own Father, making himself equal with God.

—John 5:16–18

[Jesus said,] "Your father Abraham rejoiced at the thought of seeing my day; he saw it and was glad." "You are not yet fifty years old," the Jews said to him, "and you have seen Abraham!" "I tell you the truth," Jesus answered, "before Abraham was born, I am!" At this, they picked up stones to stone him [for blasphemy], but Jesus hid himself, slipping away from the temple grounds.

—John 8:56–59

Philip said, "Lord, show us the Father and that will be enough for us." Jesus answered: "Don't you know me, Philip, even after I have been among you such a long time? Anyone who has seen me has seen the Father. How can you say, 'Show us the Father'?"

—John 14:8–9

"If you are the Christ," they said, "tell us." Jesus answered, "If I tell you, you will not believe me, and if I asked you, you would not answer. But from now on, the Son of Man will be seated at the right hand of the mighty God." They all asked, "Are you then the Son of God?" He replied, "You are right in saying I am."

—Luke 22:67–70

7. What is the strongest reason you can give for modifying or even rejecting the statements Jesus made about himself? In other words, if you believe he was wrong, why was he wrong? What would be your more accurate description of Jesus' true identity?

Titles Applied to Jesus in the Bible

Christ (Messiah). The promised deliverer-king who would rule over Israel and usher in a new age of peace. The word means "Anointed One," referring to the act of pouring oil on the head of one set apart for leadership.

Son of God. "Son of" is a phrase often used to show close identification with something. For example, Judas, the betrayer of Jesus, is called the "son of perdition" (John 17:12 in the Greek). Calling Jesus "Son of God" shows his identification with God. Jesus is also the Son of God because of the Virgin Birth (Luke 1:34–35). And he is on a par with God, unlike any other human being, because he called God his own Father, meaning that he believed he and God shared the same nature (John 5:18).

Son of Man. This was the most common title Jesus used when referring to himself. Though the term shows Jesus' close identification with humanity, its most dramatic use was when Jesus invoked it to reveal his belief that he was the "Son of Man" described in Daniel's apocalyptic vision: that "Son of Man" rules over the universe forever (Daniel 7:13–14; see also John 5:26–27). Jesus used the title this way at his trial (Matthew 26:63–65) and was condemned for blasphemy.

Son of David. King David was one of the most famous and powerful kings in ancient Israel. God promised him a descendant whose reign would never end, and this eternal King would reunite Israel and bring back its former glory.

Rabbi. Hebrew for "teacher." A term of respect, like our word *professor.*

Prophet. Anyone who speaks words directly from God. This does not necessarily involve predicting the future; a prophet need not "foretell" but will always "forth tell." Jesus did both.

I AM. A title God used in reference to himself when speaking to Moses at the famous burning bush (Exodus 3:14) and also when speaking through the prophets: "I am he" (Isaiah 43:10, 13, 25). In Hebrew, God's name, "Yahweh," sounds like "I am." Jesus used this most sacred name for himself (John 8:58).

Lord. A range of meanings, from the simple, respectful "Sir" to a way to address God himself. People meant many things in calling Jesus Lord, but Jesus made it clear he was in every way "Lord"—as much as God himself (Luke 2:9–11; Matthew 7:22–23; 12:8; John 13:13; 5:22–23; 20:28–29).

Savior. Jesus' name in Hebrew can be translated "God who saves." God was called a Savior in the Old Testament after a personal, military, or other type of victory. Jesus is our rescuer primarily through saving us from the penalty of sin (Matthew 1:21; John 1:29).

8. People sometimes allege that Jesus' followers put the words recorded in the Gospels into his mouth—that he never said the things attributed to him. What do you think of this allegation in light of what you've learned in this session?

HEART OF THE MATTER

9. What are some of the implications for all humanity if Jesus really was the unique Son of God?

10. What are some implications for your life if Jesus was God come to earth in human form? What is your emotional reaction to that idea?

11. According to John 8:24 ("I told you that you would die in your sins; if you do not believe that I am the one I claim to be, you will indeed die in your sins"), what priority did Jesus place on accepting his true identity?

12. What do you think is behind people's emotional reactions in thinking Jesus' claims are offensive? What is the hardest thing for you to accept about his claims?

CHARTING YOUR JOURNEY

With this session you're beginning a journey. Keep in mind that you do not need to feel pressured to "say the right thing" at any point during these discussions. You're taking the time to do this work because you want answers and because you're willing to be honest about your doubts and uncertainties. You may also have others in your life who would benefit from hearing about what you'll be learning. So use these sessions profitably—ask the tough questions, think "outside the box," learn from what others in your group have to say. But keep being authentic about where you are in your process.

To help you see yourself more clearly, throughout this guide you will have an opportunity to indicate where you are in your spiritual journey. As you gain more information, you may find yourself reconsidering your opinions from week to week. The important thing is for you to be completely truthful about what you believe—or don't believe—right now.

13. On a scale from one to ten, place an *X* near the spot and phrase that best describes you. What reasons do you have for placing your *X* where you did?

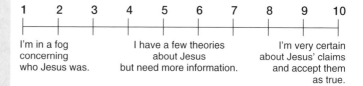

1	2	3	4	5	6	7	8	9	10

I'm in a fog
concerning
who Jesus was.

I have a few theories
about Jesus
but need more information.

I'm very certain
about Jesus' claims
and accept them
as true.

How Is Jesus Different from Other Religious Leaders?

Truth from Many Sources

Everywhere you turn, people have nice things to say about Jesus. Even those who don't call themselves his followers have profound respect for his teachings. Take for example the late Mahatma Gandhi. He wrote, "I should not care if it was proved by someone that the man called Jesus never lived.... For the Sermon on the Mount would still be true for me." Claude Montefiore, a Jew who was not a Christian, said Jesus was "the most important Jew who ever lived ... the greatest religious exemplar of every age. God's nearness was felt by Jesus directly with a vivid intensity unsurpassed by any man."

Such statements from a devout Hindu and Jew show a tolerance that's commendable. We would all do well to find the points of agreement among religions and downplay the differences.

Why can't people say nice things about every other religious leader? Sure, maybe you're most loyal to your own faith, but just as it's silly to make too much of your school loyalty, it's offensive to make too much of your religious alma mater.

Yet many people think that their religious leader is the only one from God. Why must one be right at the expense of another? Doesn't that lead to wars and intolerance? Isn't America built on the foundation of freedom to worship as you choose? So why should one way be right?

How different was Jesus anyway? Don't the great men who started religions basically say the same thing? Love your fellowman, be honest, and pay your taxes . . . things like that. As long as what these people taught is basically the same, why should we quibble over differences regarding whether this one was a guru or a prophet or just a great moral example? Such speculations just divide people and create hostility. The essence is what the leader taught—who the person was is irrelevant.

Basically, religions would be the same if none of their leaders had actually lived, because we could all just use the teachings they left behind. The sources are inconsequential.

Place Jesus up on the shelf next to Muhammad or the Buddha or Baha'u'allah. Wouldn't they get along fine if they were locked in a room together? Seeing as they probably wouldn't fight or disagree, why can't their followers stop trying to make them out to be more than they really are? Let's just boil down their teachings to essentials and stop trying to make Jesus the only one who's right or the only one who's the Son of God. Isn't that a more reasonable and practical approach to religion?

He was too great for his disciples . . . For to take him seriously was to enter upon a strange and alarming life, to abandon habits, to control instincts and impulses, to essay an incredible happiness . . .

—H. G. Wells

OPEN FOR DISCUSSION

1. Describe a time when you observed or experienced bigotry or prejudice in action. What particularly angers you about such behavior?

2. Some people think commitment to one particular religious point of view is like bigotry—a sort of spiritual prejudice. Do you agree? Explain.

3. What are some bad reasons for strong religious feelings? Describe someone you know who exhibits such unreasonable or irrational convictions.

4. Read the following statements. Put an *A* in front of those you agree with; put a *D* if you disagree.

_____ All religions are fundamentally wrong, because there is no God.

_____ Most of the great religions have at least some truth.

_____ All world religions teach essentially the same thing.

_____ Christianity is the best of all the world religions but not necessarily the only one from God.

_____ Jesus would not want sincere followers of other religions to convert to following him.

_____ Jesus believed he was more correct than other religious teachers.

_____ Jesus is the only one in all of history who has pure truth and no error.

_____ Every religious founder except Jesus was either self-deceived or knowingly fraudulent.

_____ I have solid reasons for my beliefs about the truth claims of the various world religions.

Comment on your answers.

STRAIGHT TALK

What World Religions Teach About God

There are undeniable similarities in the way world religions teach about how we should treat our fellowmen. Centuries before Jesus, Confucius said, "Do not do to others what you do not want done to yourself" — a less assertive version of Jesus' famous "Do unto others as you would have them do unto you."

Where religious leaders differ greatly is in their teachings about God and how they viewed their own roles here on earth. Jesus' uniqueness becomes very apparent when compared on this level.

5. In the following chart, the only religion completely dependent on its founder is Christianity. Do you agree that this is the case? Explain.

Religion	Founder	Role of Founder	Important Distinctives
Hinduism	None (*Vedas* collected from 1000 to 900 B.C.; *Upanishads* date from around 600 B.C.)	None	• No personal God. • An accumulation of teachings from various sources gathered over centuries; happily blends contradictory elements with little concern for resolve. • No central leader or teacher. • Millions of gods, though ultimately they (and we) are all part of the One (Brahman). • Krishna is a popular figure but not historical. • Any person can become enlightened—humans, gurus, and leaders show differences only in degree (though we're all ultimately absorbed into the Oneness of the universe).
Buddhism	Siddhartha Gautama (the Buddha; around 500 B.C.)	Enlightened teacher	• The Buddha "discovered" the Four Noble Truths about suffering and then formulated the Eightfold Path to eliminate suffering. • Buddhism is essentially a way of life that promises to eradicate suffering by overcoming human desire. • The Buddha was an agnostic in regard to belief in a supreme being. • Has much in common with Hinduism, though advocates a "middle way" between extremes of asceticism and hedonism

Religion	Founder	Role of Founder	Important Distinctives
Buddhism (cont.)			• The Buddha's teachings would be just as valid if he had never lived, because no truth is dependent on him personally; he doesn't save us, we save ourselves through applying his teachings.
Confucianism	Confucius (around 500 B.C.)	Collector of wisdom	• Has little to say about classic religious concerns. • Mostly a way to live more happily through an ideal social system (ethics); no clear teaching about the afterlife or what God is like. • Collected others' writings; wanted to be known as a transmitter rather than as an author.
Taoism	Lao-Tzu (around 500 B.C., though details of his life are uncertain)	Teacher of wisdom	• Concerned with life and health more than God. • Philosophy of life that attempts to help followers live in "the Way" (the Tao) through compliant conformity with the underlying pattern of the universe. • Has some mystical and magical elements; emphasis on simplicity and emptying oneself.

Religion	Founder	Role of Founder	Important Distinctives
Islam	Muhammad (around A.D. 600)	Prophet	• Allah is a personal God and Muhammad is his most recent prophet. • Allah would never condescend to become a man—offensive concept to Muslims. • The Koran teaches Jesus was only a prophet, like Muhammad (though Muhammad is the prophet for our age and supersedes Jesus).
Judaism	Ethnically: Abraham (around 1800 B.C.) As a religious and ceremonial system: Moses (around 1400 B.C.)	Abraham was to have many descendants to create a nation. Moses gave the Law (Torah) of God.	• Rooted in the same spiritual tradition as Christianity, but rejects Jesus' claims to be Messiah and Deliverer. • Primitive sacrificial system for sin now obsolete because of destruction of temple in A.D. 70. • Various branches of modern Judaism (Orthodox, Conservative, Reformed) differ widely in their approach to spirituality—radical monotheism is at the root of each.

Religion	Founder	Role of Founder	Important Distinctives
Christianity	Jesus (around A.D.29)	God in human form (show what God is like) Die a sacrificial death to pay for humankind's sin	• There is no Christianity without Jesus; if Jesus was not Messiah, he was an impostor and Christianity is a hoax. • Christianity is the only world religion that claims its founder is God in the flesh (not merely a prophet or guru); other religions either reject this teaching or try to make Jesus respectable by softening his claims to deity. • If Jesus didn't pay for our sin when he died, we are still unforgiven and Christianity is an empty promise of new life.

6. How different would Christianity be if Jesus had claimed only to be a prophet (like Muhammad or Elijah) instead of the Son of God?

7. Jesus made many pronouncements that sound offensive to people who want to be open to alternative points of view. Consider these few examples:

> He who is not with me is against me, and he who does not gather with me scatters.
>
> —Matthew 12:30

> All authority in heaven and on earth has been given to me.
>
> —Matthew 28:18

> I tell you the truth, the man who does not enter the sheep pen by the gate, but climbs in by some other way, is a thief and a robber.... I am the gate for the sheep. All who ever came before me were thieves and robbers."
>
> —John 10:1, 7–8

> I am the way and the truth and the life. No one comes to the Father except through me.
>
> —John 14:6

What is your explanation for Jesus' apparent narrow-mindedness?

8. Is it possible we misunderstood what Jesus meant? Explain why you think that.

9. Why do you think people try to soften Jesus' stark claims and keep some aspects of his teaching without fully recognizing his deity? Why would that be dishonest and a distortion of Jesus' message?

STRAIGHT TALK

First Person

I tried. I really tried to allow Jesus into my life without getting "fanatical." But the more I read about what he said, the more he refused to stay on the lower shelf where I wanted him on display.

In the beginning I started just accepting that he was a good man, a great teacher. His influence was undeniable — history is split by his presence on earth. What if I didn't believe in God but tried to incorporate Jesus' teaching in my life?

But how do you obey Jesus' first and most important command, to love God with all your heart and soul and strength and mind, without believing in God? Besides, what wise person gets the first principle of his philosophy wrong? That's not wisdom — that's stupidity.

So I had to believe in God to accept Jesus. But couldn't I also accept other religions? Jesus could be just one of many great teachers. Surely, he wasn't so egotistical that he had no room for teaching other than his. But as I thought about it and reread his words, I realized Jesus was concerned with idolatry. It isn't that people worship God too much; it's that their human-derived religious systems distort God. They end up with ideas about him that aren't worthy of him, and have no security upon which to build a relationship with him. People groping after transcendent deity can get only so far without getting it wrong. And then, in the name of religion, they'll do destructive things, things that God never asked, things that don't bring life, things that make God more distant and confusing. So Jesus offered clarity, not arrogant elitism. He offered solid ground to stand on in the dangerous swamp of human religious opinion.

So then, could Jesus be the most clear, the most safe — but not the only one? To believe that, I would have had to disregard the massive amount of teaching Jesus gave about himself. How could Jesus know profound truths about God and life but be mixed up about his own identity?

And there was that nagging realization that he had asked for commitment. He wanted me to love him and be loyal to him. None is worthy of our devotion as he is. If I wanted him, he allowed for no unclaimed corner of my heart in which other spiritual loves could reside. The Bible calls the church the bride of Christ. And if I took him to myself, I must take his insistence that I say, "I do" — followed by "I don't" to all other suitors. It's not that he's intolerant; he just wants the marriage to work.

So now I'm what you might call "devoted." I tried to keep my faith a weekend thing; Jesus insisted on a commitment. And I found out he's absolutely worthy of it. Now that he's got my pledge, I wouldn't have it any other way.

The Vedas said, "Truth is one, but the sages speak of it in many different ways."

The Buddha said, "My teachings point the way to attainment of the truth."

Muhammad said, "The truth has been revealed to me."

Jesus Christ says, "I am the Truth."

—"Truth Funnies: Comparative Religions in a Nutshell," a poster distributed by the Spiritual Counterfeits Project

10. What is your reaction to the above story? With what parts can you identify? Do any parts trouble you? Which ones and why?

11. As a result of this session, how would you sum up what makes Jesus different from all other religious leaders?

12. On a scale from one to ten, place an X near the spot and phrase that best describes you. What reasons do you have for placing your X where you did?

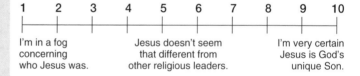

I'm in a fog
concerning
who Jesus was.

Jesus doesn't seem
that different from
other religious leaders.

I'm very certain
Jesus is God's
unique Son.

Did Jesus Really Claim to Be God?

A Grand Misunderstanding?

All the national dignitaries are present. If you hold any important political office, you are seated in the chamber. Special guests crowd the balconies. Then a shout: "Mr. Speaker, the President of the United States!" The president himself enters the room. A round of applause erupts from the floor. A simultaneously felt electric charge engulfs the electorate. This is the evening of the State of the Union address, and everybody's listening.

When the speech is done, spin doctors begin their work. What a strange range of responses! The president's political allies are ecstatic. "A fantastic speech!" they boast. "This is a great time in American history, and the credit must go to the president." But the president's detractors are many as well. They blame him for much of society's problems. "His proposals will lead to ruin," they reason, "and he didn't touch on the issues the American people want addressed."

Did these folks listen to the same message? Didn't we all hear the same words? How could there be such varied opinions about what the president meant? Clearly, it's possible to twist or interpret words however you want. This couldn't be more true than in the political realm—unless perhaps you're discussing the spiritual realm. There too spin doctors abound. They're called theologians, gurus, pastors, or psychics.

This ... raises the question whether Jesus regarded himself as in any sense a Messiah or spiritual ruler; and there is singularly little evidence in the synoptic Gospels to carry out this claim.... Jesus regarded himself as typically human, and claimed authority and regard in that respect.

—*The Jewish Encyclopedia*

They all have a take on Jesus. Here's what he really said; this is what he really meant. With four different authors giving four different slants on Jesus, they couldn't possibly agree, could they? Are these people all talking about the same guy?

And the deity of Christ is not a main focus of Jesus' teaching, either. That idea came much later. No human being would have had the gall to claim he was God incarnate—certainly not someone with the humble disposition of Jesus. Surely, Jesus never claimed anything about being God or Messiah or King; those were all titles others gave him. The people who knew Jesus couldn't possibly have heard or even endorsed such an exaggerated view of him.

But now that the accepted "party line" is widely taught, people are too fearful to challenge it. We've grown comfortable with a divine Jesus. He's everything we hope God would be, so why change our minds now—even if Jesus' statements contradict us?

What did Jesus really say about himself and his position with God? That's what we intend to discover in this session.

OPEN FOR DISCUSSION

1. When you were growing up, what were you led to believe about Santa Claus? What was the effect on you when you found out he wasn't real?

2. In your early years, what were you taught about who Jesus was? Mark your answer on the continuum below.

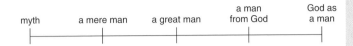

What reasons were supplied to persuade you that what you were learning was fact, not just dogma?

To get to the heart of this session, we must take a bird's-eye view of what the New Testament says about Jesus. Keep in mind that for the discussion, you do not have to agree with the statements recorded in the Bible. The important issue here is, exactly what did Jesus and those around him believe him to be? Your own opinion of whether Jesus was right about himself is a separate issue for now.

STRAIGHT TALK

Jesus Was Human

Notice how the New Testament shows Jesus' full humanity:

> He started life as a baby, born from a woman (Luke 2:6–7).
> He went through the developmental stages of childhood (Luke 2:52).
> He had a normal job as a carpenter (Mark 6:3).
> He got hungry and thirsty (Matthew 4:2; John 19:28).
> He got tired (Mark 4:38).
> He was sad (John 11:35).
> He had limited knowledge (Matthew 24:36).

He got angry (John 2:13–17).

He was terrified of his impending suffering (Matthew 26:38).

His friends disappointed him (Matthew 26:46–48).

He bled and died (John 19:33–34).

3. Why do you think the biographers of Jesus recorded details about Jesus' simple, human qualities?

STRAIGHT TALK

Jesus Was Extraordinary

Now observe some of the exceptional aspects of Jesus' life:

Jesus' birth was filled with unusual signs and wonders (Matthew 1:18–25).

Jesus showed precocious wisdom (Luke 2:41–49).

Jesus performed miracles (Luke 5:12–13).

Jesus changed lives (Luke 19:1–8).

Jesus had supernatural knowledge (John 4:16–18).

Jesus confounded his enemies (Matthew 22:15–46).

Jesus considered himself without sin (John 7:18; 8:46; 18:23).

Those around Jesus considered him sinless (except for blasphemy) (John 10:31–33).

4. Why do you think the biographers of Jesus included these details about his life?

STRAIGHT TALK

Jesus Claimed Divinity

It is sometimes asserted that Jesus was one of the most remarkable men who ever lived, but that he never claimed divinity. According to this view, people who didn't know Jesus held him in higher esteem than he ever held himself. Those with this view say Jesus never claimed to be anything more than Messiah (a prophet); it was later theologians who concocted the idea of Jesus' divinity. What does the Bible say about Jesus' views regarding his divinity?

> Jesus believed he would judge the world at the end of time (Matthew 7:21–23; John 5:22).
>
> Jesus believed he should be honored as much as God (John 5:23).
>
> Jesus believed he gave eternal life to those who came to him (John 5:21, 40).
>
> Jesus believed that to see him was to see God (John 14:9).
>
> Jesus believed that to know him was to know God (John 8:19).
>
> Jesus believed that to hate him was to hate God (John 15:23).
>
> Jesus believed he could forgive sin (Mark 2:5, 10).

Jesus accepted worship and being called "God" (John 20:28–29).

Jesus claimed titles exclusive to God (John 8:56–59).

Jesus claimed he and the Father were one (John 10:30).

Jesus believed he had been with God in heaven and shared divine glory (John 17:5).

Jesus believed he could hear and answer prayers (John 14:14).

After the Resurrection, Jesus believed he was omnipresent (Matthew 28:20; John 14:23).

5. What would you conclude if your next-door neighbor made the above claims? Explain.

6. If Jesus didn't want us to think he was God, how could he have made that clear? Do you know of any incident in which Jesus apparently tried to deny his divinity?

7. Clearly, some people find the possibility that we are a "visited planet"—that God came and lived among us—very exciting and hopeful. Yet history shows a widespread hostility to this understanding of Jesus' life. Why might this idea sometimes spark angry opposition?

8. What are the implications for your life if Jesus really was God in the flesh? What is a difficult or troublesome aspect of this truth for your life today?

9. Based on what you have discussed in this session, what would you say to someone who proposed that Jesus claimed to be only a teacher or rabbi?

10. What do you think it would take (or what did it take) for you to come to the same conclusion as Thomas and say, as he finally did, "[Jesus, you are] my Lord and my God!" (John 20:28)?

11. On a scale from one to ten, place an X near the spot and phrase that best describes you. What reasons do you have for placing your X where you did?

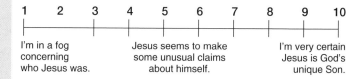

Why Focus on Jesus' Death?

A Strange Cult

At midnight the prison guard puts his security card in the slot. The heavy doors effortlessly swing open with a loud clank. He and another guard approach the cell of the condemned man. The cell door opens and the convict steps out and is led down the hall to the electric chair. "Dead man walking!" the guard somberly calls out.

Outside the prison walls a vigil is held. The condemned man's followers and loyal supporters continue to protest. "He's innocent!" they shout. "This is not justice, this is murder!"

Despite protests and last-minute efforts by the man's lawyers, no stay is granted. The phone linked to the governor's mansion never rings. The execution proceeds without incident and at 12:17 A.M. the man is dead.

But within a few months a strange thing happens. The man's supporters begin letter-writing campaigns, phone in to radio talk shows, and become very public in their enthusiasm for his cause. What is especially bizarre is that they all speak of the electric chair as if it were something great. Many of them actually wear jewelry made in the shape of an electric chair. They call attention to their leader's death as his finest hour, and in a bizarre twist, they seem to glory in the chair of death that took their leader from them.

> I would never want to be a member of a group whose symbol was a guy nailed to two pieces of wood.
>
> —comedian George Carlin

51

What would ever cause the emergence of such a weird group? Whatever it would take, that's exactly what happened in the case of Jesus. The early Christians spoke much about Jesus' death—Jesus himself anticipated it and set the course of his life resolutely toward that end. And today, all across the world, many of his followers wear the instrument of his torture and death as a piece of jewelry.

This state of affairs seems absurd. Have Christians totally lost their focus? The emphasis is in the wrong area—religious leaders should be honored for their lives and good works, not for their deaths. We need their teachings, not their tragedies. No other major world religion has such a fixation on its founder's demise. Who cares how Muhammad or the Buddha died? Certainly their deaths aren't the basis of Islam or Buddhism.

Yet Christians persist in their preoccupation with Jesus' death. Is this really the way he wanted to be remembered? How does his view of the meaning of his death compare with the current way people look at it?

What is the point of all this talk of "the cross of Christ"?

OPEN FOR DISCUSSION

1. Do you remember a time when you got into really big trouble when you were growing up? What were the consequences for you?

2. In the financial world, to forgive a debt means to cancel it—to allow the person who owes you money to be free from ever having to repay. How is forgiving someone's wrongdoing against you similar to forgiving a debt he or she owes you?

3. Sin is often compared to a debt we owe God. In what sense would offending God (sinning) create a debt to him?

4. Early in the Bible (Genesis 3:21), when the first humans commit the first sin, what does God do to show his care for them in spite of their rebellion against him? Although it was cruel and necessarily bloody, what teaching about the cost of sin might God be trying to communicate through this symbolism?

The rationale of sacrifice in general may of course throw some light on the theory of the atonement, but even so, what a primitive mythology it is, that a divine Being should become incarnate, and atone for the sins of men through his own blood!

—Rudolf Bultmann

5. Later in the Bible we see another example of how the life of an innocent animal was used to make a powerful spiritual point. What were the ancient Israelites instructed to do in Exodus 12:21–27? What lesson would the people learn about the relationship between a covering of blood and death's power?

6. The nation of Israel was struck with a plague of snakes during their time of wandering in the desert. What did God want them to do as a solution to the problem (Numbers 21:7–9)? What lesson might this bizarre episode have taught the people about the need for faith in God and about the futility of self-effort to gain God's approval?

7. Jesus referred to the above story and compared it to his own crucifixion (John 3:14–16; 12:32–33). What parallels do you see between these two events and how the benefits provided by God are received?

8. What is the purpose in paying a kidnapper a ransom? Jesus said his life would be given "as a ransom for many" (Matthew 20:28). Why would Jesus say we need to be ransomed—in what sense has the human race been kidnapped and held captive?

9. John the Baptist called Jesus "the Lamb of God, who takes away the sin of the world" (John 1:29). How is Jesus like the Passover lamb you read about earlier?

HEART OF THE MATTER

10. Some people find it offensive to place emphasis on sacrifices and innocent animals dying. What is your reaction to these historical events and commands from God?

The Bottom Line

But God is up in heaven
And he doesn't do a thing,
With a million angels watching,
And they never move a wing. . . .
It's God they ought to crucify
Instead of you and me,
I said to this Carpenter
A-hanging on the tree.

—Sydney Carter

The New Testament says God paid the debt of all your sins by substituting Christ's death for yours. He took your punishment so you wouldn't have to; he died so you could live. His sacrificial death is the pinnacle of the whole substitutionary atonement system that goes back to the beginning of human history. Other religions understand the need for sacrifices, but no other religion has God coming down to be the sacrifice. Philip Yancey put it this way: "In an incomprehensible way, God personally experienced the cross. Otherwise, Calvary would go down in history as a form of cosmic child abuse, rather than a day we call Good Friday." Frederick Buechner observed, "Like a father saying about his sick child, 'I'd do anything to make you well,' God finally calls his own bluff and does it. Jesus Christ is what God does, and the cross [is] where he did it."

11. What is your reaction to Jesus' mission of giving up his life on your behalf? Why would any story about the purpose of Jesus' life and death be woefully incomplete without this crucial point?

CHARTING YOUR JOURNEY

12. On a scale from one to ten, place an X near the spot and phrase that best describes you. What reasons do you have for placing your X where you did?

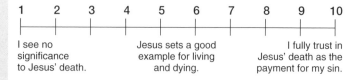

| 1 | 2 | 3 | 4 | 5 | 6 | 7 | 8 | 9 | 10 |

I see no
significance
to Jesus' death.

Jesus sets a good
example for living
and dying.

I fully trust in
Jesus' death as the
payment for my sin.

Isn't the Resurrection of Jesus a Myth?

Too Good to Be True

Over the years, many have seriously questioned the historicity of Jesus' crucifixion and resurrection. Consider the following observations from one such skeptic.

> Nothing could be more improbable than the story of Christ's crucifixion. The civilization of Rome was the highest in the world. The Romans were the greatest lawyers the world had ever known. Their courts were models of order and fairness. A man was not condemned without a trial; he was not handed to the executioner before being found guilty. And yet we are asked to believe that an innocent man was brought before a Roman court, where Pontius Pilate was Judge; that no charge of wrongdoing having been brought against him, the Judge declared that he found him innocent; that the mob shouted, "Crucify him; crucify him!" and that to please the rabble, Pilate commanded that the man who had done no wrong and whom he had found innocent, should be scourged, and then delivered him to the executioners to be crucified . . . ! A Roman court finding a man innocent and then crucifying him? Is that a picture of civilized Rome? Is that the Rome to which the world owes its laws? In reading the story of the Crucifixion, are we reading history or religious fiction? Surely not history.

On the theory that Christ was crucified, how shall we explain the fact that during the first eight centuries of the evolution of Christianity, Christian art represented a lamb, and not a man, as suffering on the cross for the salvation of the world . . . ? At the close of the eighth century, Pope Hadrian I, confirming the decree of the sixth Synod of Constantinople, commanded that thereafter the figure of a man should take the place of a lamb on the cross. It took Christianity eight hundred years to develop the symbol of its suffering Savior. For eight hundred years, the Christ on the cross was a lamb. But if Christ was actually crucified, why was his place on the cross so long usurped by a lamb? In the light of history and reason, and in view of a lamb on the cross, why should we believe in the Crucifixion?

—Marshall J. Gauvin,
Did Jesus Christ Really Live?

Even if we were to grant the possibility of Jesus being crucified, surely this business of coming back from the dead is ludicrous. How can a thinking person accept that as fact, not fiction? It strains every intellectual muscle to affirm a dead corpse living again after three days. Christianity might have had a chance to be a contending franchise in the "reasonable philosophies of life" shopping mall, but add in that resurrection stuff and no thinking person would buy it at any price. Christian teaching, with all its lofty wisdom and high ideals, looks silly in the light of the allegation that Jesus was seen up and about after he died.

Why can't we have Jesus without this foolishness?

OPEN FOR DISCUSSION

1. Describe a situation in which you were asked to trust someone who turned out not to be trustworthy. How did you feel about what happened?

2. Describe a time when you were sure things were going to turn out terribly, but somehow the outcome was much better than you anticipated. What did that happy ending do to you?

3. Jesus' closest associates (the disciples) did not seem to understand an important aspect of his mission. What does Matthew 16:21 indicate was their area of misunderstanding?

STRAIGHT TALK

Theory 1: Jesus Didn't Really Die

One way to verify the Resurrection is to propose alternatives and see if they stand up to scrutiny. Let's look at several theories of what might have happened.

Version A of the first theory — Jesus didn't really die — says Jesus was crucified but taken down from the cross before his death. After a few days of rest, he recuperated. Version B says someone else was arrested and crucified in his place, so when Jesus appeared later, it was really him — but not resurrected (this is what is taught in the Koran and believed by all Muslims).

> And their saying: Surely we have killed the Messiah, Jesus son of Mary, the apostle of Allah; and they did not kill him nor did they crucify him, but it appeared to them so . . . they have no knowledge respecting it, but only follow a conjecture, and they killed him not. Nay! Allah took him up to himself . . .
>
> — Sura 4:157–158, the Koran

4. What do you think of this theory?

Now consider the following facts.

- Jesus was pierced with a spear (John 19:34). Surely if the crucifixion hadn't killed him, that would have.
- What food and water—let alone medical attention—could he have received in the tomb? How could a man who almost died appear to be victorious and healthy three days later?
- How did such a sickly man get out of the tomb, which sealed with a large stone and guarded?
- If someone other than Jesus was crucified, what wounds did he show Thomas (John 20:27)?
- The whole of Jesus' teaching and his character crumble if he has perpetrated a hoax and

made people believe he was back from the dead when in fact he never died. A Jesus who lied is not worthy to follow.

- Where did Jesus go? The resurrection appearances stop after forty days; did Jesus go into retirement? How would such a well-known, recognized figure do that?

STRAIGHT TALK

Theory 2: Wish Fulfillment

Jesus was on record as saying that he would be killed (as opposed to taking over control of the nation and successfully ousting the Romans). He also said several times he would rise from the dead. So maybe the disciples, in their earnest desire to see their beloved Master, became self-deluded and began to see what they were hoping to see.

5. What do you think of the above theory? Does the evidence point to hopeful disciples, intent on seeing their leader again as he promised they would? Or does the record show a discouraged band of disbelievers? Notice the following texts.

On the first day of the week, very early in the morning, the women took the spices they had prepared and went to the tomb. They found the stone rolled away from the tomb, but when they entered, they did not find the body of the Lord Jesus. While they were wondering about this, suddenly two men in clothes that gleamed like lightning stood beside them. In their fright the women bowed down with their faces to the ground, but the men said to them, "Why do you look for the living among the dead? He is not here; he has risen!" ... When they came back from the tomb, they told all these things to the Eleven and to all the others. . . . But they did not believe the women, because their words seemed to them like nonsense.

—Luke 24:1–6, 9, 11

[Thomas] said to them, "Unless I see the nail marks in his hands and put my finger where the nails were, and put my hand into his side, I will not believe it."

—John 20:25

STRAIGHT TALK

Theory 3: The Disciples Perpetrated a Hoax

According to this view, the disciples stole Jesus' body and then claimed there had been a resurrection. This theory was antici-pated by the religious leaders (Matthew 27:62–66). When the tomb was found to be empty, they promoted it as the "official explanation" (Matthew 28:11–15).

6. What do you think of this theory?

Now consider these pertinent facts:

- The disciples consistently showed cowardice, not boldness. They fled when Jesus was arrested, and Peter denied him.
- The disciples weren't even expecting a resurrection—they certainly wouldn't have manufactured something they weren't anticipating.
- How could the guards have known who stole the body of Jesus if they were asleep at the time?
- If this was a conspiracy, none of the members broke under pressure—something that almost always happens when a group of people are trying to keep a secret.
- What made the disciples so bold as to preach openly in the very city where Jesus had been crucified only weeks before? Something convinced these men to put it all on the line.
- Jesus appeared to others after his resurrection, including a group of five hundred people (1 Corinthians 15:6). How could the disciples have pulled that off?
- All but one of the disciples eventually faced martyrdom rather than renouncing their belief in Jesus' resurrection. Would they have died for what they knew was a hoax?

STRAIGHT TALK

Theory 4: A "Spiritual-Only" Resurrection

According to this view, we have all misunderstood the Resurrection. It was Jesus' spiritual presence the disciples felt, and they recognized that although their leader was physically dead, his teachings lived on. He could live through them — in a metaphysical way — if only they'd let him. The Resurrection was the birth of new hope that something beyond Jesus' physical presence was available.

7. Which of the following points gives you the best reason(s) for dismissing this theory? Why does that particular point make sense to you?

- Jesus predicted a physical resurrection—that his body would rise, not just his spirit (John 2:19–21).
- The tomb was empty—what accounts for that?
- The enemies of Jesus could have easily refuted the early Christian claims by producing Jesus' body or telling people to go visit the tomb and see for themselves. Such a counteroffensive was never launched, because there was no body to view.
- A spiritual resurrection is not scandalous; many people at that time believed in life after death. What fueled the early Christians' fervor was the view that something unprecedented in history had happened. This is also what infuriated Jesus' enemies. The mere existence of Jesus in some kind of afterlife is not sufficiently controversial to explain the Jews' intense opposition, and certainly not enough to warrant Jesus' followers propagating their belief to the point of martyrdom.

STRAIGHT TALK

Additional Points to Ponder

What other than the Resurrection explains the rapid emergence of the church, poorly organized but highly infectious?

What other than the Resurrection explains the conversion of skeptics like Paul?

What other than the Resurrection explains the change of the Jewish Sabbath from Saturday to Sunday — unthinkable for devout Jews unless something very significant happened on that day?

What other than the Resurrection explains the early and repeated message that Jesus was alive, and explains why the disciples based every other Christian belief on that? ("Peter and the other apostles replied: 'The God of our fathers raised Jesus from the dead — whom you had killed by hanging him on a tree. . . . We are witnesses of these things'" [Acts 5:30, 32]; "If Christ has not been raised, your faith is futile; you are still in your sins" [1 Corinthians 15:17]; "If you confess with your mouth, 'Jesus is Lord,' and believe in your heart that God raised him from the dead, you will be saved" [Romans 10:9].)

8. Which of the above arguments seems strong to you? Explain.

> It was therefore impossible that they [the early Christians] could have persisted in affirming the truths they have narrated, had not Jesus actually risen from the dead, and had they not known this fact as certainly as they knew any other fact.
>
> —Simon Greenleaf, an authority in jurisprudence at Harvard Law School

HEART OF THE MATTER

9. Why do you think Jesus' resurrection is such an emotionally charged issue?

10. What is hard for you to accept when it comes to the subject of Jesus' resurrection?

11. What additional evidence would help you gain more certainty about the Resurrection?

CHARTING YOUR JOURNEY

12. On a scale from one to ten, place an X near the spot and phrase that best describes you. What reasons do you have for placing your X where you did?

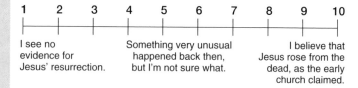

1   2   3   4   5   6   7   8   9   10

I see no evidence for Jesus' resurrection.

Something very unusual happened back then, but I'm not sure what.

I believe that Jesus rose from the dead, as the early church claimed.

?

What Impact Does Jesus Make Today?

A Force for Good?

It's sad but true that much evil has been done in the name of religion, some of it in the name of Jesus. Who among us hasn't known some zealot who was at the least an annoying turnoff and who might have actually done someone harm? If Jesus is such a good influence, why does he inspire such buffoons?

We all know the stories of the Inquisition—people being tortured if their faith didn't match up with the church's official line. Then there were the Crusades—unprovoked military aggression spurred on by the pope himself. Throughout history the divine right of kings, polygamy, and slavery have all been "proved" by Scripture. In our day the Ku Klux Klan considers itself utterly faithful to the teachings of the Bible, abortion clinics are bombed by "the Army of God," and children and wives are physically beaten with "justification" from Scripture.

If we ask for a show of hands of people who believe that Jesus and Christianity have done more harm than good, plenty of folks are willing not only to be counted but to speak forcefully. Consider the following examples.

> Of all the systems of religion that ever were invented, there is no more derogatory to the Almighty, more un-edifying to man, more repugnant

to reason, and more contradictory to itself than this thing called Christianity.

—Thomas Paine

What is the function that a clergyman performs in the world? Answer: he gets his living by assuring idiots that he can save them from an imaginary hell.

—H. L. Mencken

The Bible has been interpreted to justify such evil practices as, for example, slavery, the slaughter of prisoners of war, the sadistic murders of women believed to be witches, capital punishment for hundreds of offenses, polygamy, and cruelty to animals. It has been used to encourage belief in the grossest superstition and to discourage the free teaching of scientific truths.

—Steve Allen

The Christian religion has been and still is the principle enemy of moral progress in the world.

—Bertrand Russell

Sobering words, and there's certainly some truth to them. But do they show that Christianity's legacy is primarily useless at best and harmful at worst? Must we blame Jesus himself for these problems? Can't we find some good somewhere that shows Jesus' positive contributions?

OPEN FOR DISCUSSION

1. What are some ways you've observed people going astray in the name of following Jesus? Do you think that was Jesus' fault? Explain.

2. What are some of the good things you believe Jesus has brought to the world (even if you are not personally a believer in him)?

STRAIGHT TALK

Imagine

Imagine a world without Christian influence. Do away with every hospital that's been started by a Christian organization, every Christian relief agency, soup kitchen, child sponsorship, and school, every class that's ever been taught in a church about parenting or any other subject, every Alcoholics Anonymous meeting, every home Bible study group, every piece of art, literature, or music that has a Christian theme or source of inspiration, every sacrifice someone made because they believed God wanted them to do it, every decision that in any way was influenced by Jesus' teaching "Do unto others. . . ." Take away all the hope anyone has ever had when they prayed, remove every deed done by someone with one eye on eternity, stifle all the courage inspired by someone sensing that God was with them in spite of hardship, never let any child get tucked in with a parent kneeling beside the bed saying nighttime prayers to Jesus, demolish every church, fire every pastor who gives himself in daily service to his congregation, answer every little child's questions about God with "No one in the universe created you or loves you perfectly — you are an accidental accumulation of dust and will someday return to the nothingness you came from," teach no one any of the words left by Jesus, and allow no one to live his or her life following the pattern of the one who washed his disciples' feet.

Get rid of Jesus and that's the world you'll live in.

3. How would your life be different if there were no Christian influence in the world?

4. The big questions in life are universally believed to be

- "Is there a God?"
- "Why am I here?"
- "Where am I ultimately going?"

Based on the following passages, how would Jesus answer these questions?

Whoever wants to save his life will lose it, but whoever loses his life for me will find it. What good will it be for a man if he gains the whole world, yet forfeits his soul?

—Matthew 16:25–26

One of the teachers of the law came and heard them debating. Noticing that Jesus had given them a good answer, he asked him, "Of all the commandments, which is the most important?" "The most important one," answered Jesus, "is this: 'Hear, O Israel, the Lord our God, the Lord is one. Love the Lord your God with all your heart and with all your soul and with all your mind and with all your strength.' The second is this: 'Love your neighbor as yourself.' There is no commandment greater than these."

—Mark 12:28–31

My Father's will is that everyone who looks to the Son and believes in him shall have eternal life, and I will raise him up at the last day.

—John 6:40

I have come that they may have life, and have it to the full.

—John 10:10

5. Because Jesus answers the big questions by saying God comes first, he puts in place priorities that are different from those of the world around us. How would you describe Jesus' version of life's priorities, based on the following passages?

Jesus called them together and said, "You know that those who are regarded as rulers of the Gentiles lord it over them, and their high officials exercise authority over them. Not so with you. Instead, whoever wants to become great among you must be your servant, and whoever wants to be first must be slave of all. For even the Son of Man did not come to be served, but to serve."

—Mark 10:42–45

In everything, do to others what you would have them do to you, for this sums up the Law and the Prophets.

—Matthew 7:12

Blessed are the poor in spirit, for theirs is the kingdom of heaven. Blessed are those who mourn, for they will be comforted. Blessed are the meek, for they will inherit the earth. Blessed are those who hunger and thirst for righteousness, for they will be filled. Blessed are the merciful, for they will be shown mercy. Blessed are the pure in heart, for they will see God. Blessed are the peacemakers, for they will be called sons of God. Blessed are those who are persecuted because of righteousness, for theirs is the kingdom of heaven.

—Matthew 5:3–10

Do not worry, saying, "What shall we eat?" or "What shall we drink?" or "What shall we wear?" For the pagans run after all these things, and your heavenly Father knows that you need them. But seek first his kingdom and his righteousness, and all these things will be given to you as well.

—Matthew 6:31–33

6. Based on the passages below, how does Jesus offer help through life's hard times?

Come to me, all you who are weary and burdened, and I will give you rest. Take my yoke upon you and learn from me, for I am gentle and humble in heart, and you will find rest for your souls. For my yoke is easy and my burden is light.

—Matthew 11:28–30

I will ask the Father, and he will give you another Counselor to be with you forever—the Spirit of truth. The world cannot accept him, because it neither sees him nor knows him. But you know him, for he lives with you and will be in you. I will not leave you as orphans; I will come to you.

—John 14:16–18

Blessed are you when people insult you, persecute you and falsely say all kinds of evil against you because of me. Rejoice and be glad, because great is your reward in heaven, for in the same way they persecuted the prophets who were before you.

—Matthew 5:11–12

I have told you these things, so that in me you may have peace. In this world you will have trouble. But take heart! I have overcome the world.

—John 16:33

Surely I am with you always, to the very end of the age.

—Matthew 28:20

7. Considering the passages below, what does Jesus promise to those who place their trust in him?

God so loved the world that he gave his one and only Son, that whoever believes in him shall not perish but have eternal life. For God did not send his Son into the world to condemn the world, but to save the world through him. Whoever believes in him is not condemned.

—John 3:16–18

Do not let your hearts be troubled. Trust in God; trust also in me. In my Father's house are many rooms; if it were not so, I would have told you. I am going there to prepare a place for you. And if I go and prepare a place for you, I will come back and take you to be with me that you also may be where I am.

—John 14:1–3

I am the resurrection and the life. He who believes in me will live, even though he dies; and whoever lives and believes in me will never die.

—John 11:25–26

HEART OF THE MATTER

8. What aspects of Jesus' teaching seem to you to be too good to be true?

9. What do you think would characterize the life of someone thoroughly convinced that the things Jesus said are true and that his promises are completely trustworthy?

10. What holds you back from completely accepting Jesus' provision of forgiveness and leadership of your life?

11. What is one step you could take right now to give yourself (or more of yourself) to Jesus as best you know how, with whatever faith you have?

One Solitary Life

He was born in an obscure village, the child of a peasant woman. He grew up in another obscure village, where he worked in a carpenter shop until he was thirty. Then for three years he was an itinerant preacher. He never had a family or owned a home. He never set foot inside a big city. He never traveled two hundred miles from the place he was born. He never wrote a book, or held an office. He did none of the things that usually accompany greatness.

While he was still a young man, the tide of popular opinion turned against him. His friends deserted him. He was turned over to his enemies and went through the mockery of a trial. He was nailed to a cross between two thieves. While he was dying, his executioners gambled for the only piece of property he had—his coat.

When he was dead, he was taken down and laid in a borrowed grave.

Nineteen long centuries have come and gone, and today he is the central figure for much of the human race. All the armies that ever marched, and all the navies that ever sailed, and all the parliaments that ever sat, and all the kings that ever reigned, put together, have not affected the life of man upon this earth as powerfully as that one solitary life.

—author unknown

12. On a scale from one to ten, place an *X* near the spot and phrase that best describes you. What reasons do you have for placing your *X* where you did?

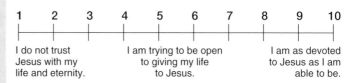

| 1 | 2 | 3 | 4 | 5 | 6 | 7 | 8 | 9 | 10 |

I do not trust
Jesus with my
life and eternity.

I am trying to be open
to giving my life
to Jesus.

I am as devoted
to Jesus as I am
able to be.

Recommended Resources

Ken Boa and Larry Moody, *I'm Glad You Asked* (Chariot Victor, 1995).

Gregory Boyd and Edward Boyd, *Letters from a Skeptic* (Chariot Victor, 1994).

William Lane Craig, *Reasonable Faith* (Crossway, 1994).

C. Stephen Evans, *Why Believe?* (Eerdmans, 1996).

Cliffe Knechtle, *Give Me an Answer* (InterVarsity, 1986).

Andrew Knowles, *Finding Faith* (Lion, 1994).

Peter Kreeft and Ronald Tacelli, *Handbook of Christian Apologetics* (InterVarsity, 1994).

C. S. Lewis, *Mere Christianity* (HarperSanFransisco, 2001).

C. S. Lewis, *Miracles* (HarperSanFransisco, 2001).

Paul Little, *Know What You Believe* (Chariot Victor, 1987).

Paul Little, *Know Why You Believe* (InterVarsity, 2000).

Lee Strobel, *The Case for Christ* (Zondervan, 1998).

Lee Strobel, *The Case for Faith* (Zondervan, 2000).

Willow Creek Association

Vision, Training, Resources for Prevailing Churches

This resource was created to serve you and to help you build a local church that prevails. It is just one of many ministry tools that are part of the Willow Creek Resources® line, published by the Willow Creek Association together with Zondervan.

The Willow Creek Association (WCA) was created in 1992 to serve a rapidly growing number of churches from across the denominational spectrum that are committed to helping unchurched people become fully devoted followers of Christ. Membership in the WCA now numbers over 10,500 Member Churches worldwide from more than ninety denominations.

The Willow Creek Association links like-minded Christian leaders with each other and with strategic vision, training, and resources in order to help them build prevailing churches designed to reach their redemptive potential. Here are some of the ways the WCA does that.

- **A2: Building Prevailing Acts 2 Churches—Today**—an annual two-and-a-half day event, held at Willow Creek Community Church in South Barrington, Illinois, to explore strategies for building churches that reach out to seekers and build believers, and to discover new innovations and breakthroughs from Acts 2 churches around the country.

- **The Leadership Summit**—a once a year, two-and-a-half-day conference to envision and equip Christians with leadership gifts and responsibilities. Presented live at Willow Creek as well as via satellite broadcast to over one hundred locations across North America, this event is designed to increase the leadership effectiveness of pastors, ministry staff, volunteer church leaders, and Christians in the marketplace.

- **Ministry-Specific Conferences**—throughout each year the WCA hosts a variety of conferences and training events—both at Willow Creek's main campus and offsite, across the U.S., and around the world—targeting church leaders and volunteers in ministry-specific areas such as: evangelism, small groups, preaching and teaching, the arts, children, students, women, volunteers, stewardship, raising up resources, etc.

- **Willow Creek Resources®**—provides churches with trusted and field-tested ministry resources in such areas as leadership, evangelism, spiritual formation, spiritual gifts, small groups, stewardship, student ministry, children's ministry, the use of the arts-drama, media, contemporary music —and more.

- **WCA Member Benefits**—includes substantial discounts to WCA training events, a 20 percent discount on all Willow Creek Resources®, *Defining Moments* monthly audio journal for leaders, quarterly *Willow* magazine, access to a Members-Only section on WillowNet, monthly communications, and more. Member Churches also receive special discounts and premier services through WCA's growing number of ministry partners—Select Service Providers—and save an average of $500 annually depending on the level of engagement.

For specific information about WCA conferences, resources, membership, and other ministry services contact:

Willow Creek Association
P.O. Box 3188
Barrington, IL 60011-3188
Phone: 847-570-9812
Fax: 847-765-5046
www.willowcreek.com

TOUGH QUESTIONS

Garry Poole and Judson Poling

"The profound insights and candor captured in these guides will sharpen your mind, soften your heart, and inspire you and the members of your group to find vital answers together."   —Bill Hybels

This second edition of Tough Questions, designed for use in any small group setting, is ideal for use in seeker small groups. Based on more than five years of field-tested feedback, extensive revisions make this best-selling series easier to use and more appealing than ever for both participants and group leaders.

Softcover

How Does Anyone Know God Exists?	ISBN 0-310-24502-8
What Difference Does Jesus Make?	ISBN 0-310-24503-6
How Reliable Is the Bible?	ISBN 0-310-24504-4
How Could God Allow Suffering and Evil?	ISBN 0-310-24505-2
Don't All Religions Lead to God?	ISBN 0-310-24506-0
Do Science and the Bible Conflict?	ISBN 0-310-24507-9
Why Become a Christian?	ISBN 0-310-24508-7
Leader's Guide	ISBN 0-310-24509-5

Pick up a copy at your favorite local bookstore today!

ZONDERVAN™

GRAND RAPIDS, MICHIGAN 49530 USA

WILLOW
Willow Creek Resources